QUIET
SEASONS
OF
Singleness

A 30-DAY DEEP DIVE DEVOTIONAL
TO BUILD CONFIDENCE IN GOD AND SELF

SARITA A. FOXWORTH

Books by Sarita A. Foxworth

Spiritual Growth

- *How to Heal a Broken Heart:* Transition From Pain to Peace
- *The Single Woman's Prayer Book:* How to Get Answers From Heaven
- *The Proverbs 31 Woman's Devotional:* 31 Days To A Renewed Mind & Spirit
- *How God Speaks:* The Ultimate Guide to Hearing From God Clearly & Consistently
- Sarita Foxworth's Faith-Based Fasting Planner

Life's Purpose and Calling

- *The Prophetic Woman:* Boldly Declaring the Word of the Lord
- *Find Your Purpose:* The Ultimate Guide to Unveiling and Stepping Into Your God-Given Life's Purpose
- *Dream Interpretation Journal:* Record Holy Spirit Inspired Dreams, Visions and Prophetic Words

Love, Dating, and Relationships

- *How to Prepare for Your Future Husband:* Waiting, Dating & Trusting God for Your Adam
- *Quiet Seasons of Singleness:* A 30 Day Deep Dive Devotional to Build Confidence in God and Self
- *Giving Birth to Miracles:* Manifesting Supernatural Childbirth
- *Smart Dating Rules for Christian Women:* Biblical Wisdom & Guidance for Love, Dating & Relationships

Book Marketing

- Attracting an Audience of Book Buyers for New Authors

To connect with Sarita or order group books and beautiful gifts for your next event visit: **www.SaritaFoxworth.com**

QUIET
SEASONS
OF
Singleness

A 30 DAY DEEP DIVE DEVOTIONAL TO BUILD
CONFIDENCE IN GOD AND SELF

SARITA A. FOXWORTH

Printed in the United States of America

First Printing, 2023

ISBN 9798385678228

Published by L & M Publishing, LLC lmpublishing.co

Table of Contents

My Prayer for You

Lord, I pray for every woman who reads this book that you bless her with an abundance of peace, joy, and patience in her singleness. Help her to understand, acknowledge and embrace your love fully. Reveal to her who you are as a loving, compassionate Father who never leaves her side. Allow her to experience the fullness of your love personally and undeniably. I ask that her purpose and calling be made clear and that you stir up the gifts you have placed inside her born-again spirit. I set myself in agreement with her greatest heart's desire—a godly marriage to a kind, loving, and spirit-filled man of God. I pray she will have a powerful testimony to share of your love and goodness as she moves through this quiet season of singleness. In the name of Jesus Christ, Amen.

Biblical Teaching on Marriage

I have embraced the calling to encourage and teach women of God who desire marriage and have conducted hundreds of Bible studies, corporate fasts, and prayer meetings curated for women who are single, but desire godly marriage.

I teach women to unapologetically walk by faith and not by sight concerning their desire for marriage. Every pro-ceeding chapter and statement of faith is based solely on the uncompromised Word of God, not mere opinion or phi-losophy. I make no blanket statements, no judgment calls, and I don't pretend to know it all. One thing has been made clear to me throughout my studies and spiritual training. **God's original plan for man and woman to be fruitful and multiply has never changed.**

When we do a full study of the Word of God, we will find a common thread woven throughout the scriptures that indeed reveals the heart of God concerning families. He has always desired a family, and a big one at that. His desire was never to have an abundance of single women and only a sprinkling of happily married couples here and there within the Body of Christ.

God's desire has and always will be to have strong, God-glorifying marriages and strong God-glorifying sin-gle persons (some who desire marriage and some who do not) to create a beautiful family of believers called the Body of Christ. For simplicity's sake, I will leave it at that. Still, I will point you to over 200 Bible Studies I have held on this topic specifically for women like yourself using the QR code below and the robust scripture list in the Appendix. Oh, how I love technology! Using the

QR code, you will find a plethora of intercessory prayer videos and topical Bible studies to give you a full understanding of your current season and desired state. Be prepared to be inspired and have your faith energized in a fresh, new way!

Sarita's Bible Study Channel

Day 1

For Most Women, Singleness is Only a Season

Genesis 1:28 (NKJV)

> *Then God blessed them, and God said to them, "Be fruitful and multiply; fill the earth and subdue it; have dominion over the fish of the sea, over the birds of the air, and over every living thing that moves on the earth."*

*L*et's start at the very beginning. What does the scripture tell us God's original plan for mankind was upon creating the very first man and woman? To be fruitful and to multiply. God didn't want us only to be fruitful and single. He wanted us to get married, be fruitful, and have children, which is literally what it means to multiply. This is a very simple concept we humans have made complicated in recent generations.

1

Think about what the Lord meant when he released that initial blessing on his first children in the Garden of Eden. He wanted them to get married, have children and enjoy this beautiful earth. He wasn't referring to them multiplying by accumulating wealth, purchasing properties, or owning multiple entrepreneurial endeavors. He also didn't mean multiplying by making disciples of Christ and winning souls into the Body of Christ, for at that time, Jesus hadn't yet been born.

God has always wanted a family. What better way for him to grow a family than for his children to have children?

One reason God's original intention for man and woman has become complicated is that some women tend to look at someone else's life and let that person's negative experience trump the Word of God. It can also be because you believe it's taking a long time for your personal prayers to be answered. Many marriages are entered into that are outside of God's will and end in divorce, creating confusion and unbelief. Not to mention the unrelenting influence of media and pop culture that makes women feel bad for expressing their personal desire for marriage and children.

But, in this moment, I want you to focus on God's words at the very beginning of mankind and consider what they mean for you personally. *Be fruitful and multiply.*

Singleness is only a season for those of us called to enter into the beautiful union of a godly marriage in our future. While in this single season, we should focus on being as fruitful as possible and trust in God to connect us with our purpose partner in due season.

How do you grow in fruitfulness? You begin working on yourself inwardly so that you can become a greater blessing outwardly. Share the love of God and make as many disciples of Christ as possible. Bless people everywhere you go, even those who are the hardest to love. Love them anyway.

Preach about the first and second coming of Christ. Win as many souls into the kingdom as possible.

Flourish and blossom as a woman. Treat your mind and body well. Set and reach personal and professional goals regularly. It feels so good to make progress! Become so financially prosperous you can follow in the example of our father in the faith Abraham—become blessed to be a blessing.

Give from the abundant supply only heaven can produce in your life. Give love, food, hugs, favors, clean water, shelter, and smiles. BE Christ to this lost world and bring them into the kingdom of God. This is what fruitfulness looks like. It's spreading and growing as deeply and richly as possible in your own unique way.

Don't allow this season of your life to be wasted with idle thoughts and engaging in pointless debates about dating, love, and marriage. Rest assured in God's faithfulness and trust in his will to sustain your heart during the waiting and bring you into the fantastic promised land he promised you personally.

Selah—What ways are coming to mind for how you can grow in fruitfulness? How will focusing on growing in fruitfulness help you to be more patient in singleness?

Simple Prayer

Father, I ask that you help me to understand your personal plan for my life. Reveal more of the remarkable woman you created me to be and the incredible works you are calling me to do. In Jesus' name, Amen.

Embrace Your Desire

Proverbs 10:24 (AMPCE)

The thing a wicked man fears shall come upon him, but the desire of the [uncompromisingly] righteous shall be granted.

*Y*our innermost desires are hand-selected and imparted by God himself. I am not talking about worldly or surface-level desires. But the desires that are a part of your spiritual makeup, filled with intricate detail and specificity, perfectly woven together, curating the master-piece of the woman you are.

Take a moment and think about who God is. He is the Almighty, All-Powerful, Sovereign One. When he breathes life into a creation, it's with great thought and intention. He didn't just string you together haphazardly. Psalms 139:13-16 gives us a bit of information about how God formed our intricacies since before we were in our mother's womb.

5

He had thoughts and plans for our individual lives even before he masterfully created us.

When you learn more about the magnificence of the mind of God through different creations, you will easily accept that your desire for marriage was placed within your heart by the hand of God Himself. How else would you get such a great and significant desire?

Godly marriage is not merely about gratifying the flesh. Marriage, for a kingdom woman, comes with an immense purpose, duty, and responsibility. It's such a great calling that it was the first assignment given to the very first woman God created. He didn't tell her first to learn who she was, minister, start a business, launch a non-profit, serve the community, work her way through the corporate ladder, and then, finally, after she lived a full life to get married. The Lord created Eve, spent personal time with her (while Adam was still sleeping), then later brought her to Adam for marriage and purpose fulfillment.

Your desire for marriage is beautiful. It is from God. That's why you can't pray it away. It's a calling. It's not an evil, carnal desire. It's a desire birthed from love for the purpose of love.

The struggle you are having is with the time it's taking. Or, perhaps, you made a wrong turn in life and have veered off course from God's plan. Or, maybe you've been on the right path, serving, seeking, fasting, praying, and living holy, yet still...you're single.

The trials of faith and your personal journey do not determine who God created you to be or what your calling is. God determines who you are created to be and what your calling is. The clock and calendar don't decide whether God's plan for your life has changed or not. God decides.

Simply put, if God has placed the desire to be a wife and possibly a mother within your heart, then that's what he also wants for you. Don't allow the clock or external influences to discourage you or bring confusion or doubt. Press into God and learn more about your desire and how he wants your life to bring him glory while single and waiting, and then once you are found by the man you're praying for.

Reflective Bible Study:

Over the next three days, read all the scriptures you can about desires. Write down the answers to each question once you have read through all the scriptures.

- What is the common theme you notice?
- What is the requirement or process found preceding the desires being given by God?
- What do you believe the main takeaway for you personally should be regarding your desire for marriage?
- What are some ways you can make peace between having the desire and waiting patiently on God?

Simple Prayer

Lord, I ask for a deeper revelation about my desire for marriage. Show me what purpose you have for me to fulfill right now as a single woman, and teach me how to embrace the desire for marriage without allowing the desire to consume and frustrate my heart, mind, and emotions. In Jesus' name, Amen.

Trusting God with Your Desire

Psalms 20:4 (NLT)

*May he grant your heart's desires
and make all your plans succeed.*

Psalms Chapter 20 is one of my favorite chapters to cross-reference with Psalms 37. Both chapters speak about God's trustworthiness, faithfulness, and saving power. Not only will he rescue you from all harm and danger, but he will also give or grant you the desires of your heart. So you are not limited to only expecting God to help you when you're in trouble, but you can trust him with your other desires and petitions.

In other words, you don't have to figure out how, when, and where you're going to meet that amazing man, date, court, marry and raise a family. The scripture tells us that God is there to assist and even coordinate the process.

As usual, there are some prerequisites on our part. We are to delight ourselves in the Lord, give offerings, totally trust and rely on God and have an effectual prayer life (all of which are laid out in both chapters). And, as we pray, serve, give and enjoy our single lives with God, he will bring to pass our deepest desires.

Your single season is quiet right now, but that doesn't mean nothing is happening. We are not meant to know or see all that God is doing. We are meant to trust and have faith, believing in what we cannot see. Human nature is to want to know everything that is happening and control some of the details. Yet, God's nature is that we follow his lead, not the other way around.

There are times when you will need to encourage yourself as David did. Sing and shout praises to God because you know victory is assured. Worship God with your all and trust him, even in those hardest, most confusing moments of singleness.

When you trust God, you won't continually question his timing. When you trust God, you may want to fuss at God with your words, but you will actually pray and make requests with thanksgiving to God. When you totally rely on God, you will not take matters into your own hands, believing (falsely) that you can control the outcome.

Press in with prayer, service, and worship. Give your absolute all to your God-given purpose and assignment. Learn more about the nature of God, the workings of the Holy Spirit, and the person of Christ. This is how you trust in God with your actions as well as your words.

Selah—Why do you find it hard to trust in God? Do you believe he loves you? Do you believe he is all-powerful? Do you believe your desire for marriage is from him?

Simple Prayer

Lord, help me to rest in faith, knowing assuredly that you are trustworthy and faithful. Teach me more about your love and how I can walk more closely with you in this quiet season. In Jesus' name, Amen.

Hidden by God

Job 1:10 (NLT)

You have always put a wall of protection around him and his home and his property. You have made him prosper in everything he does. Look how rich he is!

God's protection is a blessing. Yet, during quiet seasons when you are not being approached or asked out on dates or when all the wrong types of men are approaching you, you don't feel blessed. You feel invisible. You feel ignored. By men and, sometimes, even by God.

You may have been doing all the "right" things but seem to be getting no closer to marriage or a real, solid relationship.

It's during these times that I believe you are in "The Safe" with God. God's safe is a private, protective space where he keeps his most valuable possessions. There is nothing more valuable to God than his children. Your value in the eyes of God is priceless. He does not want any man enjoying your company who is not worthy of loving you properly. He also does not want any man to come into your life that could potentially damage your heart and spirit.

So he keeps you safely tucked away in this blessed, safe space. Think about the differences in the various levels of quality in jewelry. Does costume jewelry belong in a safe? No. Are precious stones and fine jewelry left out on the open shelves of retail stores? No.

You are not off-the-rack costume jewelry available for any and everyone to try on, touch, fondle, or even steal. You are like a rare, precious stone, kept in the special safe in the back of the jeweler, that is only accessible by lock and key or secret code. Only those who can afford your high price AND are willing to pay that price are able to see you and have the opportunity to experience the blessing of your conversation and company.

In this season, God wants you all to himself right now. He does not want you distracted by many ill-intentioned men. He wants you focused on your relationship with him, your purpose and calling, and becoming the kingdom woman he envisions you to be.

The Lord knows that the right attention from the wrong man will steal your attention and heart away but will not lead to the godly marriage you desire. He knows that you are easily distracted by good-looking men filled with potential. He also knows how susceptible you are to demonic deception that could cause you to become backslidden, broken-hearted, or end up with an ungodly soul tie.

And what about the men who approach you who are nowhere near the type of man you are praying for? The Lord fully expects you to give them no access to your heart; he trusts you enough to use your discernment and walk away when all signs reveal this man is not the one. Keep in mind that you are a beautiful woman with an even more beautiful spirit. Your radiance will attract any man (even those who are in darkness) to seek your attention. This type of pursuit does not mean God wants you to settle or that you are being too picky. It simply means you were super cute when you left the house that day. It could also mean that Satan knows your past; he knows what you like and continually tries to distract you and prevent you from growing with God (1 Peter 5:8).

God is protecting you in this season. Don't despise your heavenly protection, Woman of God. Embrace it! Allow God time to continue to mold and develop you into the perfect wife, helpmate, and missing rib for an amazing man. Allow God time to continue to mold and develop your future husband into the powerful and strong man of God the Lord requires him to be for your home.

Selah—What do you believe God is perfecting in and through you during this season while he is keeping you hidden?

Simple Prayer

Abba Father, I thank you for divine protection during this quiet season. I believe you know what's best for me, and I trust your timing. Help me to maintain patience, trust, and focus as I await my greatest heart's desire. In Jesus' name, Amen.

Scripture Reflection

Psalms 37:3-5 (NKJV)

Trust in the Lord, and do good;
Dwell in the land, and feed on His faithfulness.
Delight yourself also in the Lord,
And He shall give you the desires of your heart.
Commit your way to the Lord,
Trust also in Him,
And He shall bring it to pass.

When you meditate on this scripture, what do you believe the Lord is speaking to your heart?

....

....

....

....

....

....

Combatting Fear and Worry

John 14:27 (NLT)

> "I am leaving you with a gift—peace of mind and heart. And the peace I give is a gift the world cannot give. So don't be troubled or afraid."

Fear is the greatest enemy of your faith. You cannot afford to allow your mind to live in a place of worry and fear; it steals your peace of mind. Jesus left us great peace because he knew we would need it.

Jesus knew that when we make firm decisions to stand in faith and face tests and trials, we would need peace, only acquired through the Holy Spirit, to keep us from becoming anxious and fearful. He knows your end from the beginning. He knows every path you will take in life and each turn along the way. He knows the length and obstacles that will arise in the waiting season.

Therefore, it's only at the feet of Jesus that the peace you need to calm an anxious heart and emotions is found. When you feel worried and afraid, run to Jesus. Don't sit and stew in distress or allow your emotions to be overwhelmed with fear. The supernatural peace of Christ will gird you up and carry you through quiet and sometimes lonely seasons.

In the first book of Peter, 5:7 tells us to give all our cares and worries to God because he cares for us. God cares about what you care about. He cares about the anxiety you feel at the thought of your prayer for marriage going unanswered. He cares about the worry you feel as you grow older and begin to wonder if and how you will bear children. God loves you, and your emotions do matter to him.

You can trust that God will help you when you are feeling overwhelmed with emotion. You can trust Jesus to help when you come to him with your cares and frustrations. You can trust that supernatural peace is easily accessible to you at the feet of Christ.

Selah—How often do you run to Jesus when your heart is feeling overwhelmed with emotion?

Simple Prayer

Lord Jesus, I come to you today, casting all my fear and worry about my singleness onto you. I ask for strength to persevere in faith without ever growing weary. I receive the gift of supernatural peace you have available for me as I await answers to my heart's prayers. In Jesus' name, Amen.

Calming an Anxious Spirit, Heart, and Mind

Philippians 4:6-7 (NKJV)

> 6 Be anxious for nothing, but in everything by prayer and supplication, with thanksgiving, let your requests be made known to God; 7 and the peace of God, which surpasses all understanding, will guard your hearts and minds through Christ Jesus.

Isn't it interesting how during a quiet season, it seems as if heaven is silent, yet everything else around you starts talking loud and clear? The people in your life questioning your singleness are loud. The thoughts in your mind when you see yet another engagement on social media are loud. The emotions inside tugging at your heart when you see a new mom brimming with joy holding her beautiful newborn baby. Or when you're the only single mom at your kid's basketball or soccer game surrounded by cheering moms with husbands actively engaged with their children. Sometimes it feels like the world is not-so-quietly suggesting that you are incredibly behind in life and missing out on a fantastic experience far out of your reach.

All of these voices and external factors only feed fear which breeds an anxious heart, mind, and spirit. This is why it is extremely important to find peace, solitude, and rest supernaturally. For it is only by the supernatural power of God, by way of Jesus Christ through your born-again spirit, that you have a shield (a guard) put up around your heart and mind made up of totally supernatural peace. The kind of peace that makes no sense at all but causes your heart and mind to trust in God no matter the circumstances or what seems to be working against your prayers and faith.

This supernatural peace of God will quench the fiery darts of anxiousness intending to short-circuit your faith. A hidden key for accessing this supernatural peace is found in contentment.

The scripture says to make your prayers and supplications known, with thanksgiving to God. You must have a thankful heart and attitude, which is the fruit of genuine contentment. You should be content knowing that your life is complete; you are a whole woman, even while you await godly marriage. You're blessed. Your body is healthy, your finances are doing well, and you eat and live well. You're not half of a woman because you're not married. You're not any less valuable because you have not yet experienced motherhood. It's possible to be content while praying for greater.

Gratitude Challenge:

This 30-day challenge will increase your peace and promote restful sleep. At the end of each night, right before you go to sleep, write down at least three things you are grateful for and thank God for each item individually. Each night, list fresh items that are not repeated from any preceding evenings.

Simple Prayer

Father God, help me to access and dwell in the supernatural peace available to me through Christ Jesus. I give you this anxious heart, and ask that you fill my heart and mind with faith, hope, and trust in you. I believe you always have and always will take care of my every need, hope, and desire. In Jesus' name, Amen.

Trust In the Vision God Gave You

Habakuk 2:3 (NLT)

This vision is for a future time.
It describes the end, and it will be fulfilled.
If it seems slow in coming, wait patiently,
for it will surely take place.
It will not be delayed.

Think about the purest vision of what godly marriage is. The agape love of God being shared between a husband, a wife, and children is truly beautiful. The glory of the Lord is revealed when there is harmony in the home, one vision of love, worship, prayer, and raising children who love and fear God as a priority. This love is poured out as this family shares with the world the same unconditional love that is exchanged within the home. As a result of this godly marriage,

Christ's love is spread, and lost souls are won into the kingdom. People who crave love and are searching for answers will find love and truth from families filled with the Holy Spirit and have agape love threaded throughout their actions.

Where does the Bible define this vision of godly marriage? Throughout the Old and the New Testament, you will find examples and solid instructions from God on how to relate to one another within a family covenant.

The Lord has always desired a family of his own from the beginning of time. He created humans to be his children and left it up to us to love him with our own free will, and to birth more loving children, we would teach about God and set the example of how to live a life of worship.

Can't you see, Woman of God, the vision you have of your own godly marriage is God's vision too? It was his vision first. The confusion arises when you consider things such as heartbreak, ungodly soul ties, divorce, lack of godly parents and leadership within the home, lack of understanding of what true agape love is, prolonged seasons of singleness, and quiet seasons of the unknown, much like what you're experiencing presently. Yet even with all these obstacles to manifesting the vision of godly marriage, God's original intention and purpose for you have not changed.

No one knows the exact timing of when any prayer will be answered. People who pray for healing want to heal instantly. People who pray for financial increases want to receive a check in the mail the next day. People who pray for their family members to become saved truly desire spiritual transformation to happen as quickly as possible. No one wants to wait for any vision.

But you can't focus more on the clock than on the promise. You can't focus more on the length of the waiting season than on maximizing each day of your life in purpose and enjoyment. You can't focus more on past mistakes than on your blessed future.

Habakkuk Chapter 2 gives us both instructions and promises for visions that come from the Lord. The main take away is to believe and run toward the vision, even if it seems delayed or it's taking a long time. The vision will be fulfilled in the future; you just don't know the exact timing. After all, God is the omniscient one, and we are his children. Our job is to believe.

Life Application:

The questions you have about the length of your wait, troubles you experienced as a child, trials you've experienced in relationships, or any personal difficulties in your singleness, should all be taken directly to your heavenly Father in quiet moments of true worship and prayer. Make quiet time to dialogue with the Holy Spirit and allow him to minister to you. You may not get all the answers to your questions, but you will acquire peace, understanding, and a supernatural rest that will fortify your faith and strengthen your resolve.

Simple Prayer

Father, I pray that you will begin to reveal to me your personal vision for my life concerning marriage and children as I study your Word and seek your Presence. Give me clear guidance and direction so I may persevere in faith with a greater understanding of this special season. In Jesus' name, Amen.

Entering Into Restful Patience

Hebrews 6:12 (NKJV)

> —*that you do not become sluggish, but imitate those who, through faith and patience, inherit the promises.*

*Y*our spirit is already equipped with all the patience you need for any promise from God that requires your faith and endurance. When you access this patience, you will also enter into a quiet, restful place spiritually. It's not hard to access this patience. The key is to build your faith to a place where your spirit gracefully enters the rest of God, and you begin to experience a restful, patient, and peaceful mind and spirit.

When you read this scripture, it can be easy to believe that through faith and patience, you can inherit the promises of God, such as healing in your body, protection from danger, or financial breakthrough. But when it comes to marriage, did God promise you a husband?

Let's take a moment to help you find peace and end the confusion of this popular question.

God's promises are threaded throughout the scriptures, from health to long life, to eternal life. Although these promises are clearly stated, humans will still debate each promise and conclude that there is no promise at all. We can see this because even though the Bible promises us the gift of eternal life only by salvation through acceptance of Jesus Christ as our personal Lord and Savior, many still believe there is another way to get this gift of eternal life or that there is no heaven at all.

But, if you are a woman who believes in the infallible Word of God as truth and the final authority, you believe in all the promises clearly stated within the Holy Bible.

The question is, are there other promises in addition to the written Word? Does God make personal promises to his children? Or is his will one-size-fits-all? Does he speak to us individually, by way of the leading and promptings of the Holy Spirit? Or, has the Lord only spoken as the Bible was written, and he is silent today?

The Lord still speaks to us today. Jesus Christ said, "My sheep know my voice," and Romans 8:14 says that we should be led by the Spirit of God. There are many other places that teach about the Holy Spirit guiding us in this lifetime, but for simplicity's sake, think about those things you have heard the Lord speak to you during your personal prayer time. What life has he shown you? What plans has he revealed to you as you study the Word, seeking guidance, direction, and confirmation? Has he promised you will be supernaturally healed from a sickness or disease attacking your body? Has he promised a financial breakthrough amid a trying situation? Did he promise to bring love and peace into your family where there has been strife and turmoil? These are all personal promises that are rooted in the Word of God.

Not everyone struggles with health challenges, financial obstacles, or broken families. So when the Lord speaks to you or gives you a vision that applies to your unique situation, this is a personal promise.

Now, what has the Lord spoken to you about a husband and marriage? What scriptures minister to you deeply about your desire for marriage as you study the Word? When you flip through your prayer journal(s), what personal revelations has God given you concerning this desire?

Restful patience is attainable when you have faith in God's personal promises to you and don't attempt to control the circumstances of the "how" and the "when." Believing what the Lord has told or shown you are first and foremost. You risk becoming impatient when you struggle with unbelief, just like Abraham's wife, Sarah. She was tired of waiting on God and decided to take matters into her own hands, which didn't turn out so well. The fruit of her labor did not lead to her and Abraham obtaining the promise. Thank goodness for Abraham's faithfulness. Since he never gave up, he could inherit the very thing God promised him—a son who would be part of the beginning lineage of Jesus Christ.

Selah—What has been attacking or undermining your faith in God's personal promises to you? How can you begin proactively mitigating and removing challenges to your faith and patience?

Simple Prayer

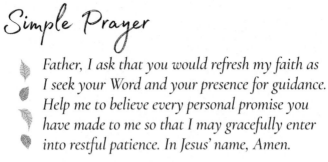

Father, I ask that you would refresh my faith as I seek your Word and your presence for guidance. Help me to believe every personal promise you have made to me so that I may gracefully enter into restful patience. In Jesus' name, Amen.

Day 9

You're More Patient Than You Realize

Romans 8:24-25 (NLT)

We were given this hope when we were saved. (If we already have something, we don't need to hope for it. But if we look forward to something we don't yet have, we must wait patiently and confidently.)

If you are experiencing prolonged singleness, I know you are a patient woman. You are more patient than you realize. Patience has proof. Your lifestyle and dating choices are proof of your patience.

When you are patient, you stick to your standards and allow God's Word to direct your actions in a relationship. The fact that you don't date non-Christians because you refuse to be unequally yoked reveals your patience. The fact that you have made a firm decision to wait until marriage to have sex with your man reveals your patience and your self-control.

If you lacked patience, you wouldn't wait on God to send you a man you are equally yoked with; you wouldn't wait for marriage to have sex, and in fact, you would take the entire dating and relationship process into your own hands, being led only by your flesh, will, and emotions.

So you see, you *are* a patient woman. When your emotions are weak, and you have some negative thoughts about your singleness, that doesn't mean you are being impatient. Thinking about your desire for a family or wondering when God will make it happen doesn't mean you are impatient. Or, when you express these emotions or thoughts verbally, it does not mean you lack patience. It simply means you are human.

Be encouraged today; you are more patient than you realize. Even if you happen to be in a place where you have made some poor choices and given your heart to the wrong man, the fact that you are ready to repent, heal and start over reveals that you have the resilience to get back on the path of patiently trusting God for love.

Even during this quiet season of singleness, you have decided to continue to work on yourself and strengthen your faith rather than throw in the towel and give up. God doesn't want that for you. He wants you to endure and manifest the most beautiful blessing possible. Continue to stand firm in patience. God is faithful!

Selah—What bad relationships have your patience and trust in God protected you from entering? On the other hand, what type of situations or relationships have you experienced due to impatient decision-making?

Simple Prayer

Lord, I ask that you fortify my patient heart and mind so I may endure this quiet and prolonged season of singleness. I refuse to waiver and place my faith firmly in your power and in your personal promises to me. In Jesus' name, Amen.

Day 10

Building Unshakeable Confidence in God

Matthew 6:33 (NKJV)

But seek first the kingdom of God and His righteousness, and all these things shall be added to you.

W hen you live your life adhering to the two principles in Matthew 6:33, you will build unshakeable confidence in God. You will find it much easier to trust God for marriage and rest during the wait. You will not feel as anxious and uncertain about your future. As a matter of fact, you will have a greater understanding and clarity about God's plan for your life, including your personal calling to a godly marriage.

The first principle in this scripture is to seek first the kingdom of God, which literally means to align your life with God's kingdom as defined in the Word of God (not speculation or opinion). What is God's kingdom? If you think about what a kingdom is, it is a population under the rulership and subjugation of a king. The kingdom follows the king's rules and plans and submits to his authority and leadership. As God's children, we are his population and should align our lives with his rules, plans, authority, and leadership. The Holy Spirit helps us to make day-to-day decisions, but most of God's rules are clearly laid out in the Holy Scripture. Even his ultimate will for man is clearly stated in Genesis Chapters 1 and 2.

We have the life of our Lord Jesus to use as our foremost example, in addition to other great spiritual leaders in the Bible. Jesus Christ also left us more insight and governance on whom to serve, minister to, and how to live our lives as born-again Christians in these last days. God's kingdom is clear. It includes various instructions, guidance, and rules such as service, giving, the fruit of the Spirit, personal relationship with Christ via the indwelling of the Holy Spirit, prayer, faith, walking in the love of Christ, and much more.

The second principle in Matthew 6:33 is that of seeking his righteousness. Now, what is the righteousness of God? Genesis 15:6 lets us know that Abraham was righteous because he believed God. Romans 3:22 lets us know that we are made righteous by faith in Jesus Christ. It's not enough to have knowledge of Christ alone. You must also *believe* in him.

You must believe that Jesus Christ is your Lord and Savior. You must believe in the power of his resurrection unto salvation. You must believe that Jesus loves you and is always with you. This belief, this incredible faith in Christ, makes you righteous. Seeking Christ's righteousness *is* seeking Christ. To learn from him and to be more like him.

Most women have read this scripture and believed they were in total fulfillment simply because they serve in the church and study their Bible regularly. These things are great, but that is not the fullest expression of the practical application of this scripture. When the fullest expression is obtained in daily living, confidence in God begins to grow and flourish. Your confidence becomes unshakable. You know that God will give you what you need and want because you are truly seeking God's kingdom and his righteousness.

Perfection is not required to be in fulfillment of Matthew 6:33, but you do need to give your best effort. Refocus and seek the Lord with loving fervency when you fall off track. You will have a powerful testimony of how God has added the things you desire in life for his glory.

Seeking God Challenge:

Begin to study what it means to be a part of God's kingdom in this generation. When you read Bible stories, how do they apply to your life today? When you find instructions in scripture, ask the Holy Spirit to help you apply that instruction to your daily life. Seeking the kingdom of God and his righteousness is a life-long endeavor, but for now, build your understanding through intentional study and acquire personal guidance from the Holy Spirit.

Simple Prayer

Lord, I ask that you help me to better understand what your kingdom is in this generation and the role you want me to play within your kingdom. Show me how I can become more Christ-like in my daily choices, activities, and behaviors. In Jesus' name, Amen.

Scripture Reflection

Psalms 145:19 (NKJV)

He will fulfill the desire of those who fear Him;
He also will hear their cry and save them.

When you meditate on this scripture, what do you believe the Lord is speaking to your heart?

....

....

....

....

....

....

....

....

The Cure for Hopelessness

Romans 15:13 (NLT)

I pray that God, the source of hope, will fill you com-
pletely with joy and peace because you trust in him.
Then you will overflow with confident hope through
the power of the Holy Spirit.

Hope is extremely powerful. Having faith is to be assured of those things that you hope for. Without hope, there is no faith. We each desire something from God and then place our confidence in God's ability to manifest that "thing" in our lives. These desires are the very foundation of hope.

You cannot afford to allow your soul to become hopeless for marriage or any other desire in your heart. Hopelessness and despair were never in the plan of God for his children.

You were designed to live by faith, hope against hope, and testify of God's faithfulness when it's all said and done.

Even when the odds look like they are stacked against you, remain in hope. Failed relationships, struggles to break ungodly soul ties, silent dating seasons, scary doctor reports, and the lack of available spiritually-mature men are all odds that attempt to move you from hope and faith to fear and worry.

Romans 15:13 lets us in on two key insights in continuing in hope with joy and peace. These are that God is the source of hope and that it is by the power of the Holy Spirit that you obtain confident hope. Isn't that something? You don't get a small portion of hope just to barely believe God may or may not do something you desire. You receive a confident hope that God can do it, and he will!

Since God is the source of hope and since you must obtain confident hope directly from the Holy Spirit, if you find yourself feeling hopeless, this is a clear sign that your relationship with God isn't as strong as you need it to be.

Here's an example: If you were dehydrated and needed water, it would be great to be near a water well. Yet you need more than just knowing the well exists to hydrate your body. You need to go towards the well and utilize a bucket to draw the water close to you for drinking. The water well is the source of water, just like God is the source of hope. You receive water from the well by drawing it out using a bucket, just like you draw hope from God through the Holy Spirit. Drawing hope from God requires a relationship. Head knowledge alone will not hydrate a thirsty body, just like awareness of God's existence will not feed a hopeless spirit.

You must continually seek the God of Hope and take hold of the confident hope available through the Holy Spirit. The beautiful part is that this hope is coupled with joy and peace. God always provides more than we need to live by faith. In this case, he not only gives us hope so powerful that it can overcome obstacles or quietness confidently, but he gives us a joyful heart and peace of mind in the waiting season. God knew we would have to wait, and he made accommodations for us because he loves us very much.

Hope Challenge:

Over the next seven days, begin seeking God daily for confident hope in godly marriage and children. Just ask for it and pray the simple prayer below. As you believe more and become more hopeful, write down the personal revelations you receive from the Holy Spirit about your singleness and future marriage.

Simple Prayer

Father, I ask you for an abundance of confident hope for every prayer request and desire of my heart. I pray the Holy Spirit will strengthen my confidence in you and fill me until I am overflowing with peace, joy, and belief. In Jesus' name, Amen.

Day 12

Hope Building—God's Personal Promise to You

Romans 4:18 (NLT)

> *Even when there was no reason for hope, Abraham kept hoping—believing that he would become the father of many nations. For God had said to him, "That's how many descendants you will have!"*

*N*ow more than ever, It is extremely important to focus on the Bible's teachings and not drown in the world's philosophy or examples that contradict the Word (such as people who are allegedly in faith but never inherit the promises of God). You must prioritize studying and meditating on Bible stories, specifically of those people who desired a godly family, such as those you're in faith for.

Using God's Word, you will find simple, hidden treasures that can greatly bless your life if you allow the Word to take hold of your mind (having the mind of Christ—1 Corinthians 2:16) and your emotions (having the fruit of the Spirit—Galatians 5:22-23).

Consider the father of our faith, Abraham (Romans 4:16), who is described as a man who believed God, had faith in God, and hoped against hope (Romans 4:18). What was God's promise to Abraham? A godly family filled with a magnificent purpose (Genesis 12:1-3). God's promise was also filled with personal instructions for Abraham to follow in manifesting this promise, which is important to note.

We read Abraham's story (in Genesis Chapters 12-25) and see a man with astonishing faith, hope, and trust in God, which appear unsustainable in modern society. But what was the foundation of Abraham's faith? Another man's life? A syncretized philosophy of "feel-good" messages from a famous so-called spiritual person? No. Abraham's faith was in God's personal promise to him.

He didn't even have a Bible like we have today. There were no mega-churches and daily devotionals to guide him through understanding God's truth. There was also no Holy Spirit indwelling Abraham to lead and guide him in his daily choices.

Abraham was not influenced by social media, reality TV, everyone's worldly or wrongly-divided perspective or men who were in "faith" but were left hanging, sad, and mad at God. However, Abraham did have a few influences you may be able to relate to.

He had the same ticking clock to contend with. God promised him a child at 75 years old. Can you imagine waiting 75 years to hear God speak to you with a promise of something so coveted as a family? It's not like Abraham was born again at 75 years old. He had a lifestyle of worship and honoring God. On top of this, he had to wait another 25 years after God had spoken until Sarah gave birth to Isaac. That's 100 years of waiting for a desire to be fulfilled!

Another negative influence Abraham had was his wife's pessimistic attitude towards God (Genesis 18:12-15). How many voices in your life laugh at what you believe and bring doubt and confusion into your mind— even though they may claim to be well-intentioned?

The main takeaway from this brief synopsis of Abraham's faith was the importance of having a personal relationship with God so that you may HEAR his personal promise for your life. I am sure you have read many scriptures about having faith, but many people overlook the strength of listening to what God has personally shown you about your own life, not what others think, say, or want you to believe.

What has the Lord personally promised you, Woman of God? If you don't know or are not sure, be like Abraham and create a lifestyle of true worship. Spend a season focusing more on your relationship with Christ than a relationship with a man or entertainment.

Here's the great thing about God. He didn't only speak to Abraham one time. He reminded him of his personal promise to him again and again. This means God will speak to you more than once because he loves you, and he wants you to trust in him, even when all odds are stacked against you. The Lord wants you to be in hope and faith, not doubt and fear.

Make a choice, just like Abraham did, to believe what the Lord has spoken to you, no matter how long the wait is.

Hope Building Challenge:

Personalize Romans 4:18 and read it aloud:

Even when there was no reason for hope, (insert your name) kept hoping—believing that (she) would (insert God's personal promise to you). For God had said to (her), "(insert the exact words God has spoken to you)." For the next 21 days straight, read this personalized scripture aloud. Be still and quiet immediately after, and listen for any additional encouragement or instructions the Holy Spirit speaks to your heart. Even if you hear the same thing repeatedly, remember that this is the exact way he spoke to Abraham to keep the promise fresh in his mind and heart.

Simple Prayer

Lord, I ask that you would increase my spiritual sensitivity and help me to hear from and discern your spirit. Help me to receive encouragement and confirmation direct from the Holy Spirit as I await your promise for my life. In Jesus' name, Amen.

Hope Building—Pressing In When God Seems Silent

Psalms 145:19 (NLT)

He grants the desires of those who fear him;
he hears their cries for help and rescues them.

I firmly believe that the Holy Spirit is always speaking, and our Abba Father has much to say to us about our lives. But there are seasons when the Lord seems silent because of the state of our mind, heart, spirit, or emotions. Or, this can happen if you're in such a busy season that your prayer time begins to dwindle. And when you do enter into worship, you feel rushed, unable to "soak" in the presence of God to receive all the information, insight, and spiritual revelation he has for you.

There are other times when your desire seems to "scream" from within your soul, drowning out all reason, overcome by the frustration of the wait. I believe Hannah was in this spiritual and emotional state when she cried out to the Lord, year after year, for children, and those prayers remained unanswered. Hannah's story can be found in 1 Samuel Chapters 1 and 2. we can learn a lot from a woman whose desire was so strong she couldn't discern God's voice, yet she never gave up petitioning God for her deep yearning to become a mother.

Her story is a great example to follow when you have not heard from the Lord personally, yet you know deep within your heart that your desire for marriage is from God. Hannah was a worshipping woman of great faith. Her story is filled with strong emotions and external influences that tried to convince her to give up on God, yet she refused and continued to pray fervently about her desire for children.

Many faith-less Christian women would want you to believe your desire isn't from God or that just because you have a desire doesn't mean God wants that desire to manifest in your life.

If that were the case, Hannah's story wouldn't be in the Bible at all. Her story is not about how she received a prophetic Word, was moved by the Holy Spirit in a church meeting, or had an angelic visitation from heaven that she would give birth to a great Prophet. Her story is purely desire-based. She desired children, remained in faith, and God answered her prayer (simply put).

Indeed, Hannah was taunted by a carnal woman about not having children, trying to drive her into jealousy and despair—but it didn't work. Even her own husband, Elkanah, tried to convince her that she should be satisfied with him alone as if a husband and a child were interchangeable. This is similar to how people will try to convince you to be satisfied with Jesus as your husband when a relationship with Christ and a relationship with a husband are two distinct experiences. In Hannah's case, Elkanah could not convince her to settle, even though he was well-intentioned.

There was a great shift in Hannah's attitude and understanding in her final prayer requests to God when she made a personal vow filled with kingdom purpose and blessing. She promised the Lord that her child would not be hers, but he would be given back to God to serve him all the days of his life. This promise from Hannah was no small undertaking.

Today we have the privilege of physically raising our children in God's ways and teaching them personally how to love, serve and worship Jesus. But in Hannah's day, the child had to be raised miles away from home by the priest Eli, who was the only person who could raise and teach him in the ways of the Lord. Remember, this was before Jesus died on the cross for our sins, before we were filled with the Holy Spirit and before there was any Bible available in our language. Can you imagine praying for a child for years and then having to drop him off with the priest when he was only a toddler? Yet, Hannah was willing to make this sacrifice (much like Abraham was willing to give up his only, long-awaited son Isaac), and as a result, her prayers were answered.

Now I know what you're thinking. "Sarita, God, knows that my heart is in his hands, and my marriage would be his. God knows that I truly desire to honor him with my marriage. God knows that if he sent me a husband, we would do great things in the kingdom!" However, you might not have the full revelation of exactly what *your* marriage would be like if you truly gave God full control. Ask the Lord to reveal to you what it would look like if you "gave" your marriage to him versus if your marriage only belonged to you, fulfilling personal and worldly desires.

Lastly, when you read through Hannah's prayer of praise in Chapter 2 of 1st Samuel, don't just skim over the words quickly. You can gain great insight into Hannah's personal knowledge of who God is and how loving, compassionate, strong, merciful, and faithful he is for his children. She developed this great knowledge and understanding of who God is as she awaited her prayers to be answered, not *after* God gave her a child. Is your personal relationship with God growing and maturing over the years, even as you await the answer to the prayer for your greatest heart's desire?

Selah—Are you willing to wait as long as it takes to enter into a God-glorifying marriage that lines up with the roles and responsibilities of godly couples as defined by scripture?

Simple Prayer

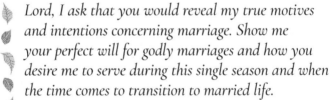

Lord, I ask that you would reveal my true motives and intentions concerning marriage. Show me your perfect will for godly marriages and how you desire me to serve during this single season and when the time comes to transition to married life.
In Jesus' name, Amen.

Day 14

Hope Building—Your Age Does Not Determine God's Will

Numbers 23:19 (NLT)

> *God is not a man, so he does not lie.*
> *He is not human, so he does not change his mind.*
> *Has he ever spoken and failed to act?*
> *Has he ever promised and not carried it through?*

*I*t's impossible for God to lie. Two wonderful cross-references to Numbers 23:19 that confirm the unchanging nature of God concerning a personal promise are Habakkuk 2:3 and 2 Peter 3:9. The Lord loves you so much. He does not make a personal promise to you, reveal his plans and purposes for your life to you, only to change his mind. If God has spoken to you about your future, the only thing that can change the will of God is if you operate in outright disobedience and refuse to live within the parameters of Christian living clearly defined in the Word of God.

My guess is if you're reading this devotional, you are a woman who loves God and is doing your best to live a life that pleases your God. You are not perfect; none of us are. Yet you strive to maintain your relationship with Christ and obey the leadership of the Holy Spirit in your daily choices. Your heart is pure. You pray for others, study your Bible, and attend church services. Even when you hit a rough patch in life, you have never stopped believing in God's love for you and have never stopped trying to do better.

The question most of us wonder is: if God wants me married, why is it taking so long? You might wonder after you have reached a certain age if God's plan for your life has changed or if you have missed God altogether. I mean, really, how hard is it for God to allow you and your dream man to cross paths?

Prolonged seasons of singleness can be rough, but be encouraged, Woman of God. God's personal promise to you will come to pass, even if it takes longer than you would prefer. I am a practical teacher, so I won't pretend that the desire to birth children naturally isn't impacted by very real bodily changes. And even if you find yourself in a season where it is not physically possible to give birth to children naturally, that may or may not change if and how you can be a mother. But when it comes to marriage itself, there is not technically any such thing as "running out of time." You may not manifest this great desire in your 20s, but even if it happens later in life, you must trust that God knows what's best for you and your future husband.

Your age is not a determining factor in understanding God's will for your life. The only thing that determines

God's will is God himself. You gain insight into his plan and purpose for your life as you grow in your relationship with him, and he unveils his personal promises to you. Once he reveals those things, your job is to patiently endure the season of waiting, remaining steadfast in the faith, and pursuing God's love and righteousness.

I have heard women tell me so many times that "Since I'm 40 years old, God doesn't want me to get married," or "I have waited for over 20 years to find love, and I am still single, so God must want me to remain single forever," or "I'm no longer able to have children, so God's will for me is to be single and love only him." If I were to inquire about the faith of these women earlier in life, they would have given me a different perspective on their singleness. They would have all believed God wanted them married, they would have been more trusting in God's revealed promise for marriage, and they would have been hopeful that it would happen one day soon.

The only change between their past and present seasons of discouragement is their age and the length of time they have been single and unmarried. This is why the focus cannot be on your age or how many years of singleness you have experienced; the focus must be on what God has personally spoken to you.

Using our father in the faith, Abraham, we can see how it looks when someone is not deterred by age but believes God no matter what. We can also look at other stories of older couples who had children, and the Bible defines them as old, such as the Shunammite woman and her unnamed husband and Zechariah and Elizabeth. These couples may have wondered about the length of time they were in faith also, but they endured until God granted their heart's desires.

The key is understanding exactly what the Lord has personally promised you concerning marriage. If it's within God's will for your life, just like Abraham, Jacob, and even Joshua, God will speak to you about how he wants to bless you more than once. He will continue to encourage your heart through the years as long as you remain in his presence with an open heart to receive his ministry. The Lord will make it clear to you exactly what his will is for your life as long as you continue to live for and with him. It's not about your age. It's all about his promise.

Selah—What has the Lord spoken and confirmed for you regarding your desire for marriage? Have you noticed any patterns, repeated revelations, or instructions? If you compile all the messages from God, Bible study revelations, prophetic words, visions and dreams, and what you believe deep down within your spirit, what exactly has God promised you?

Simple Prayer

Father, I ask that you continue to confirm and clarify your will for my life. If you desire me to become a godly wife, help me to endure this season, no matter how long it takes to come to pass. In Jesus' name, Amen.

Scripture Reflection

Jeremiah 1:12 (AMPCE)

Then said the Lord to me, You have seen well, for I am alert and active, watching over My word to perform it.

When you meditate on this scripture, what do you believe the Lord is speaking to your heart?

....

....

....

....

....

....

....

....

Day 15

Aligning Your Life With God's Will

Proverbs 19:21 (AMPCE)

Many plans are in a man's mind, but it is the Lord's purpose for him that will stand.

When God has a plan for our life, it's coming to pass. That is, as long as you remain in his presence, submitted to the Word, and following the promptings of the Holy Spirit. You don't have to live a perfect life, but when you do your best to please God and be like Christ, you will continually align your life to God's will.

The question that plagues the minds of many single women throughout the Body of Christ is, "How do I know if it's God's will for me to be married?" I have a simple answer based on what Proverbs 19:21 plainly states. If the desire for marriage and the vision in your heart for godly marriage is withstanding the test of time, that is God's purpose for you. To remain in faith until such time when God sends your husband is evidence of God's will. If you could easily walk away or forget about a fleeting desire, hope, or wish, this is a sign that the path or thought is not in alignment with God's will for your life.

Remember that season when you got tired of waiting, and you tried to pray the desire away? Remember that failed relationship where you tried to make it work with a man who was far from God? Remember when you tried to convince yourself that you had the gift of singleness because everyone around you seemed to get married first or younger? Of all these plans and paths in your mind, God's purpose is the only one that has withstood the test of time. *Your desire for marriage is still there.*

And not just any marriage. Your desire to live a life pleasing to God and marry a man with whom you can worship and raise children who are on fire for God has remained through all the trials, tests, mistakes, and prayers to remove this desire.

When God calls you to a certain life, no matter how long you ignore the call or work in disobedience, the lingering desire and heart pull remain. God's will for your life was determined even before he knit you together in your mother's womb (Psalms 139:13). Unless you decide to turn your back on God completely, his will for your life remains unchanged, no matter how much you run from it.

The first step to aligning your life to God's will is to accept God's will and embrace his purpose for you. Most times, his will makes no human sense. His thoughts are higher than ours, so the path to his purpose unfolding will be filled with bumps in the road and rocky detours. Most times, you will not be able to see clearly the path ahead or the steps to take in accomplishing his will. And faith will always require patience and waiting for an unknown period of time. This is why faith is required in our lives as Christian people. No matter what plans you make, God's will *will* prevail as long as you keep trusting, submitting to, and following him.

Submission Challenge:

Think about how you have been running from God or ignoring his calling in any area of your life. What would it look like if you stopped waiting for perfect conditions, all the answers, or a complete understanding of the full picture to move forward by faith? Over the next 21 days, make a decision to radically obey God. Step out in faith and pursue those plans and ideas he has placed in your heart that seem too scary or hard to do. Trusting him fully, take bold faith steps every day. After 21 days, you will have found a new door or opportunity on God's path to purpose.

Simple Prayer

 Lord, I ask for clarity concerning your will for my life and that you show me what real trust and faith in you look like through action. Help me to operate as a woman of great faith, trusting your plan and purpose for my life. In Jesus' name, Amen.

Finding Personal Meaning in Singleness

Proverbs 19:21 (NLT)

You can make many plans, but the Lord's purpose will prevail.

Single Christian women in this generation are stronger, more driven, and more powerful than ever. We used to dream of breaking through glass ceilings in traditional corporate environments, and now we are thriving entrepreneurs, heads of agencies, and leaders in politics, ministries, and community organizations. We still face obstacles and limitations due to gender, but we have made great strides in the last 50 years.

So if I were to ask you if you had a plan for when you wanted to be married and how many children you planned to have by a certain age, you would have a very real answer for me. You may have added that husband and 2-3 children to your vision board or your 5-year life plan, along with your supporting scriptures, seeds of faith, declarations, and even measurable steps in achieving your marriage and family goals. Driven women often have everything planned out and find it hard to imagine the possibility of things not going according to plan.

Yet, for all of our detailed planning and faith declarations, the timing is still entirely up to the Lord. Just as the Lord has purposed for you to be married in a specific season only known by the Almighty Himself, he has also given you meaning in the waiting season of singleness.

There is much for you to do, accomplish, learn, pursue and obtain. First Corinthians 7:34 tells us that unmarried women should spend this season devoted entirely to God in body and in spirit. That's the meaning of this season. God's personal will and purpose for you in this season is revealed in both your physical holiness (abstaining from all sexual activities until marriage) and your acts of spiritual worship (relationship with Christ and reverence of the Lord). This scripture also encompasses how you honor the Lord with your lifestyle and acts of service to others.

Living a life totally devoted to God is preparation for your future season of dating, love, and marriage. There is great meaning in learning who God is and how He operates, loves, and gives. There is great meaning in keeping your body holy so that you do not end up in an ungodly soul-tie and can keep a clear head in love and dating. Meaning is also found, of course, in learning who you are as a woman, seeing yourself as God sees you, and becoming crystal clear about your personal calling and anointing.

Selah—When you think about where you are spiritually, professionally, relationally, financially, and physically can you honestly say each part of your life has been devoted entirely to God?

Simple Prayer

Father, I ask that you would reveal with great clarity what purpose you have for my single season. Show me what plans you have for me and where you want me to place my focus and energy in total devotion to you. In Jesus' name, Amen.

Understanding Your Significance

Ephesians 2:10 (NLT)

> *For we are God's masterpiece. He has created us anew in Christ Jesus, so we can do the good things he planned for us long ago.*

You are not alive by accident. The Lord did not accidentally save you and bring into the truth of His glorious son Jesus Christ for no reason. He saved you, delivered you, and filled you with his precious Holy Spirit for a very significant reason.

Significance can be defined as *being noteworthy, having a particular meaning, or having a noticeable influence*. Think about it. Your life has meaning, and you have influence when you are operating in your purpose and unapologetically fulfilling your calling.

Being a masterpiece is not the same as being a piece of print artwork or a mass-produced piece of pretty decor.

For something to be considered a masterpiece means the artist took their time. They were particular in creating a dynamic piece of work that could not be duplicated; otherwise, it would lose its value. Creating a masterpiece takes thoughtful time and consideration. Every detail is planned, organized, and hand-crafted for perfection. You are God's perfect masterpiece!

Being one of God's masterpieces means your life, Woman of God, has a powerful significance. Your life is needed in this crazy world. Your voice is needed. Your service and ministry are needed. Your prayers and prophetic utterances are needed. Your acts of love and kindness are needed. Your sound Bible teaching is needed. Even your smile, personality, creativity, and artistic ability are needed.

There are good things your life was created to produce both while single and even after you are married. Your brilliance is needed in every room, environment, and space you enter. You will notice that as soon as you embrace your authentic self and show up confidently, the lives around you are blessed. You were born to be a blessing, which is easy to do when you are just being yourself.

Selah—Have you lacked confidence or self-efficacy in any area of your life? Why? What can you do to overcome this low self-confidence?

Simple Prayer

Lord, I thank you for creating me beautifully, brilliantly, and wonderfully. I love the woman I am because you love me just as I am. I ask for a greater understanding of the good things you have masterfully created my life to bring to fruition. In Jesus' name, Amen.

Day 18

Excelling in Your Life's Purpose

Matthew 28:19-20 (NKJV)

> *"Go therefore and make disciples of all the nations, baptizing them in the name of the Father and of the Son and of the Holy Spirit, teaching them to observe all things that I have commanded you; and lo, I am with you always, even to the end of the age." Amen.*

Understanding your life's purpose and finding meaning in singleness are interrelated, but they are two different experiences. Your life's purpose is the overall impact the Lord created you (specifically) to make, using your unique voice and spiritual gift makeup to save lost souls, bringing them into the glorious light of the gospel. The meaning you have in singleness is that God wants you to focus your time and energy in devotion to him while you do not have to split your time and energy with a husband and children. You will still be devoted to God once you're married, but your ability to give to God will drastically change once you are needed to care for an entire family.

Discovering your life's purpose is a huge conversation, but for simplicity's sake, put together the Great Commission (Matthew 28:19-20), the greatest commandment (Matthew 22:37-40), and Christ's life (synoptic gospels) as an example, and then think about what this all means for your personally. How specifically can you practically preach the gospel of Christ and win souls into the kingdom in your own way? How can you practically share the love of God in the greatest capacity possible with your life? How can you practically imitate the works of Christ, operating in your own gifts, teaching with the love of God, and ministering to those in need?

Once you have taken the time to conclude how you can be of the greatest use in the kingdom of God, now imagine how you can create the widest reach to maximize your impact. This world is filled with those looking for an unapologetic voice to follow and a leader to learn from. People are searching for love and answers. You will never have all the answers, but you do have some answers. You have some solutions to help people in a real way. This world needs your passion, love, and service.

Today I want you to consider how you can move beyond simply discovering your purpose to excelling in purpose. Ministry and service are so fulfilling and will help tremendously with peace and contentment in quiet seasons of singleness. The beauty in your life's purpose is that it doesn't need to look like anyone else or follow in anyone else's footsteps (except Christ, of course). You can be uniquely you, making the greatest impact only you can make operating in your authenticity.

Life's Purpose Challenge:

Look at your vision board or your written vision. If you don't have one, spend one evening writing down what you believe God is calling you to do with your life. Then, take the entire vision to the next level in your mind, and visualize making an even greater impact than you have already planned. What would it look like if you could have the farthest reach and launch the greatest ministry possible? Write it all down and upgrade your vision board with a bigger vision.

Simple Prayer

Lord, I ask that you place a greater vision in my heart for purpose and calling fulfillment. Show me the harvest as white as snow that I am uniquely created to serve. Help me see and believe the vision so I may run with it. In Jesus' name, Amen.

Creating Consistency and Focus

1 Corinthians 15:58 (CEV)

*My dear friends, stand firm and don't be shaken.
Always keep busy working for the Lord. You know
that everything you do for him is worthwhile.*

*Y*ou can experience greater contentment and peace by creating a life filled with a consistent focus, working for and with the Lord. Great joy and peace come when you consistently do your best in your walk with Christ. You will see yourself growing closer to God, becoming more spiritually sensitive, and understanding spiritual matters on a deeper level. You will notice that the same distractions that would throw you off track previously do not even phase you anymore. Personal pride will begin to grow when your spiritual growth is evident, and you can show others how to face and overcome challenges and grow in Christ.

In addition to the beautiful fruitfulness you experience in spiritual growth, you will also notice yourself growing in the anointing. Your calling and purpose will become more clear. As you begin to step out with your specific message, voice, and ministry, you will see lives changing all around you as you serve with and for the Lord. Service to God produces magnetic energy that brings people into your life who you are hand chosen to bless in your own special way. This service adds a fulfillment to your life that is felt on the deepest levels of your spirit and soul.

I have found that when a woman struggles with being consistent either in her walk with Christ or in her service to God, it's because she either lacks vision or doesn't have a full understanding of what the obtainment of that vision truly means. In other words, she lacks significance and purpose. You are significant, and your life has a purpose. Pray today's prayer to help you unlock and understand the powerful woman of God you are created to be.

Consistency and Focus Challenge: Over the next seven days, begin to jot out your "whys" each day in your prayer journal. Why is it important that you grow spiritually? Why is it important that you become a more fruitful woman? Why do you need to make more disciples of Christ as aggressively as possible? Why has God chosen you for a special work?

Simple Prayer

Lord, I ask that you help me to be more consistent in my spiritual growth and service to you. Help me focus on those things of great importance in the kingdom of God. Remove any and all distractions from my life and bless me with a greater support system for this season of my life. In Jesus' name, Amen.

Scripture Reflection

Hebrews 12:11 (NLT)

No discipline is enjoyable while it is happening—it's painful! But afterward, there will be a peaceful harvest of right living for those who are trained in this way.

When you meditate on this scripture, what do you believe the Lord is speaking to your heart?

....

....

....

....

....

....

....

Soul-Care, Not Just Self-Care

1 Thessalonians 5:23 (AMPCE)

And may the God of peace Himself sanctify you through and through [separate you from profane things, make you pure and wholly consecrated to God]; and may your spirit and soul and body be preserved sound and complete [and found] blameless at the coming of our Lord Jesus Christ (the Messiah).

Soul-Care is extremely important in this season of waiting. Living a sanctified lifestyle that is pure and consecrated to God brings great peace not known by those who allow the world to consume their souls.

When the world begins to consume our souls, it brings confusion, doubt, and fear. You begin to mistrust yourself and distrust God. You may start to second-guess God's love for you or if you are even worthy of the type of love you are praying for. When your mind is filled with thoughts that oppose the word of God, your spirit and soul become weighed down with hopelessness and despair.

You can avoid this pitfall by remaining pure, holy, and sanctified in Christ Jesus. Your soul will not become entangled by an ungodly soul-tie when you choose not to have premarital sex (of any kind). If you've experienced the hurt and devastation that follows a broken relationship filled with lust and sex, you know how it feels when the flesh consumes your soul instead of being full and free with the Spirit.

The Bible is clear about God's stance on sexual immorality. Yet, many Christians fit into the world's standards of love and dating with sex-filled relationships on the path toward marriages riddled with sin. There is no peace when you know in your heart that you are behaving outside God's clearly stated Word. If your spirit still senses conviction when you have a mere thought of sin, that is a good thing. The Holy Spirit is still trying to help you live in alignment with the Word now that you are a saved woman (Ephesians 2:1-5).

Another huge contaminant to your soul as a single woman is the strong opposing opinions of the world around you that contradict God's Word. Arguments that ensue based on beliefs such as living together unmarried, what it truly means to be unequally yoked, if it's okay to marry and date a non-Christian, and the relinquishing of household spiritual leadership from the man to the woman, all create strongholds of confusion in the mind and ultimately the soul if left unchecked.

To care for your soul means to limit the amount of ungodly influence and counsel you allow into your life so that you may remain focused on the kingdom of God and strong in your faith in God. There indeed, are those in your life who will not understand the path of consecration and holiness you have decided to live. But God is calling you to live an uncommon, extraordinary life for his glory.

If your soul has begun to feel weighed down by the cares of life and is heavy with negative thoughts and emotions, check out the things you have been feeding your soul. Examine your lifestyle and your obedience to the conviction of the Holy Spirit. None of us are called to live a perfect, pristine life. But we should all do our best to allow the Lord to lead us through his Word and Spirit.

Soul-Care Challenge:

Take a moment and examine your soul's three elements—your mind, will, and emotions. Write down what you believe has been the greatest negative influence on your soul in your current season. Then write down the greatest positive influence on your soul in this current season. What do you believe God is telling you to change, remove or avoid to bring your soul greater peace? How can you commit to following the Holy Spirit's leadership over the next 30 days to live a more consecrated lifestyle of holiness?

Simple Prayer

Lord, I committed on the day of my salvation, when Jesus became the Lord of my life, to allow you to be my master, ruler, and controller. Help me live a lifestyle aligned with your plans and purpose for my life. In Jesus' name, Amen.

Breaking Relationship Cycles

James 1:6-8 (NLT)

6 But when you ask him, be sure that your faith is in God alone. Do not waver, for a person with divided loyalty is as unsettled as a wave of the sea that is blown and tossed by the wind. 7 Such people should not expect to receive anything from the Lord. 8 Their loyalty is divided between God and the world, and they are unstable in everything they do.

When you focus steadfastly on God, the Word, and your purpose, it is easy to break relationship cycles. You will not find yourself going through a revolving door of failed relationships or meaningless dates with spiritually immature men when you make the firm decision to learn God's Word and submit fully to it.

Even though you love God, you may not be loyal or totally devoted to him. It's easy to locate where you are by first examining your actions while dating or in a committed relationship. Do you allow God's Word to take precedence in your decision-making? Or do you allow your flesh, your personal will, and desires, or the man you love to determine your choices and behaviors?

Each time I have coached or ministered to a woman who was experiencing the same negative patterns in relationships or was hopeful yet stuck in a relationship that was so obviously not God's will for her life, she was always allowing her behaviors, thoughts, and choices to be governed without total submission to God's clearly-written Word.

For example, a woman would remain in a negative relationship cycle with a man she has been having a sexual relationship with for years outside of marriage and struggles to break ties with him to end the cycle. God has repeatedly and clearly stated throughout the Word that we should not be lustful or sexually immoral. Yet the woman would refuse to place God's Word above all and choose to live in sin instead, experiencing this cycle and praying that God will intervene and make this relationship godly.

Another example is a woman who claims she believes the role of a husband as clearly stated in Ephesians Chapter 5, yet will falsely believe God wants her to date and marry a non-Christian or a man who is immature spiritually and could not lead and love a family the way God describes: as Christ loves the church.

You may be in a quiet season of singleness because God is looking for true devotion and submission to him. Because the Lord is all-knowing, I believe he protects many of his daughters by teaching them how to submit first to him before they can submit to an earthly husband. If one moment you submit and the next you compromise on God's Word, you are unstable and double-minded.

The wonderful part about breaking relationship cycles is that when you decide to date and enter a relationship while totally devoted to God, there is great peace and joy. The guilt of sin is absent, the questioning and confusion of watering down the Word are also non-existent, and you can rest and trust in God.

The promise stated in James Chapter 1 is that when you have faith in God and are completely loyal to him, you can expect to receive blessings and answers to prayer.

Selah—Do you feel stuck in negative relationship cycles? Can any of these outcomes be traced back to behaviors that opposed God's Word and will?

Simple Prayer

Abba Father, today I ask for your help aligning my desires and actions to your Word, which is your will for my life. Show me how to break free from all negative relationship cycles and enter true rest and peace while waiting for marriage. In Jesus' name, Amen.

Healing and Letting Go

Psalms 147:3 (AMPCE)

> *He heals the brokenhearted and binds up their wounds [curing their pains and their sorrows].*

God loves you, and he cares about the condition of your heart. He is near to the brokenhearted and is ready to heal, remove pain, and make you feel better by tending to your wounds. This healing provided by the Lord is a process that doesn't happen overnight but through your continued pursuit of his love.

There are many moments where I have cried in the presence of God on the heels of a failed relationship, heartbreak, and devastation. Many prayers were barely audible because of the crying out and weeping to the Lord. Especially when my heart was broken, and I experienced heart-shattering pain in the depths of my soul.

Slowly but surely, God helped me get back on my feet and understand more about his love and who I am as a woman so that I came out each time stronger than I was before those relationships started. I did not come out of those seasons bitter, jaded or angry at God. I came out better, stronger, more resilient, and more focused.

There is supernatural healing available for you too. You must continually seek the Lord in prayer, searching the scriptures, asking for his help, and believing he is always available to help. Personal worship is the act of seeking and pouring out your faith and deepest emotions to God. It's beautiful, and it is the birthplace of a renewed relationship with him.

It does not matter what mistakes you have made or how far you have strayed from godliness. The Lord still desires to heal your heart. It doesn't matter how rebellious or disobedient you were to end up in a situation. God's will has been and always will be for you to become a whole, fruitful and blessed woman.

This quiet season of singleness is the perfect time to examine your soul for any remnants of hurt and pain from the past. Or, if a recent situation is still causing you great pain, this is the perfect time to experience another level of God's love through healing and comfort. You can be comforted by friends, family therapists, and counselors, but there is no greater comfort than what's available through personal prayer and worship to and with God.

The Lord knows all. He knows you perfectly and every inch of your born-again spirit, mind, and soul. He also knows what transpired in your relationship. He can and will minister to you better than any human on Earth. If you need help healing and letting go of the past, seek the Lord continually, he will bless you!

Healing Challenge:

Over the next 30 days, spend at least 20 minutes in prayer and worship, seeking the Lord for supernatural healing. Be sure to write down anything you believe His Spirit speaks to your heart. You will have a greater understanding of your personal situation and the magnitude of God's love for you as he begins to express himself through forgiveness, comfort, and peace.

Simple Prayer

Lord, I ask that you reveal any area of my heart and soul that is broken and that you would heal me supernaturally as I continually seek your presence. I thank you for helping me let go of the past and focus forward on the beautiful future you have in store for me. In Jesus' name, Amen.

Day 23

Fearlessly Receive God's Love

1 John 4:18 (AMPCE)

18 There is no fear in love [dread does not exist], but full-grown (complete, perfect) love turns fear out of doors and expels every trace of terror! For fear brings with it the thought of punishment, and [so] he who is afraid has not reached the full maturity of love [is not yet grown into love's complete perfection].

When you pray to your Heavenly Father, what are you afraid to ask for? What area of your life or love life do you feel you ask or expect too much from God? Are you basing your prayer requests on your past and present behavior? Are you adjusting your requests to make them more reasonable, considering your disobedience or fear of God? I am not talking about the healthy, reverent fear of

God, but the fear that God is somehow punishing you for past mistakes.

Have you been single for so long that you are becoming afraid to voice your greatest desire for marriage, for fear that it will never happen? Or are you decreasing your prayer requests because you're afraid it's not God's will for you to have a happy, godly marriage?

These questions are food for thought but also help you locate where you are in fully comprehending and receiving the fullness of God's love for you. If you're scared or downright terrified of approaching God or of what you think his response might be to your requests, you still have room to grow and mature in God's love.

But what does it mean to mature in God's love?

It means to believe in God's limitless, all-consuming love for you, personally, as his special daughter, love that is unearned. He loves you regardless of your mistakes. He loves you despite your weaknesses. And he longs to bless you beyond measure.

God's love for you is evident if you take a moment and reflect on his goodness, mercy, favor, and protection for you over the years. How many times did he rescue you when you felt trapped? How many doors did he open that should have remained shut? How many situations has he brought you through? What accident or trauma was avoided without explanation? Those incidents that were supernatural for which you can only give glory to God expose his deep, unfailing love for you.

But God's love for you is so much greater than your human mind can fathom because he is much greater in wisdom and thought than we will ever be.

Get honest about why you are afraid and remove any terror of punishment or fear from your heart. Talk it all out in the presence of God. And worship him. Receive his love and expect his glory to be revealed in your life in fresh and new ways.

Comprehending God's Love Challenge:

Get a blank journal, or use your prayer journal. Write out every situation God has brought you through, whether you had to ask for his help or not. Write down every answered prayer when the situation appeared to be dire or desperate. When you were at your lowest, darkest moment and God delivered you, write them all down. When you needed God to come through, else there would have been greater devastation, write those situations down as well. Then, take a moment to reflect and thank God for helping, rescuing, delivering, providing for, and protecting you. Right at this place of deep worship, make a faith-filled, bold request without holding back.

Simple Prayer

Abba Father, tonight I receive your love anew.
Teach me more about your love for me and help me
grasp the full comprehension of your unfailing love.
Tonight, I make a bold request of ....
I ask for this because you love me, and I know
you desire to bless me beyond measure.
In Jesus' name, Amen.

Day 24

Fearlessly Love Again

Isaiah 41:10 (NLT)

Don't be afraid, for I am with you.
Don't be discouraged, for I am your God.
I will strengthen you and help you.
I will hold you up with my victorious right hand.
Don't be afraid to love again, God is with you.

*Y*ou may be divorced. You have had your heart broken into what feels like a million different pieces. Maybe the men in your family who were supposed to love and protect you did the opposite. You may have experienced hurt, trauma, abuse, neglect, unfaithfulness, or downright deception at the hands of someone who claimed they loved you. Or, maybe they didn't even pretend to love you, but because of their role in your life, you expected to be loved but instead were left hurting and broken.

These situations were in your past, and I pray you've had time to heal. Only by the power of God and in receipt of his love can you heal even the deepest wounds. Once you have received this supernatural emotional, mental and spiritual healing, it can be difficult to step out in faith and trust a new man with your heart.

But be encouraged and know that God is with you. You are not on this journey alone. You are not figuring everything out with no support. You have the Word of God as your foundation and the Holy Spirit of God inside your born-again spirit, who leads and directs your paths with great discernment to keep you out of harm's way.

You are not alone, and you don't have to repeat mistakes from your past. If you feel you keep making the same mistakes in romantic relationships and ending up with hurt feelings or, even worse, a broken heart, try something different this season. You may need to step outside your comfort zone because you attract and give your heart to the wrong men. On the other hand, you may need to be more uncompromising in your standards because when you relax those standards, you end up in the wrong situations the Lord never intended you to be in.

The key to fearlessly loving again is knowing you can trust yourself *because* you trust God. Because you trust and submit to God's Word, you know that you don't have to fornicate to get or keep a relationship. Because you trust in God's spirit and follow his leadership daily, you build friendships in new circles God is exposing you to as he orders your steps to new, unfamiliar spaces and environments. Because you trust the indwelling of the Holy Spirit, you are aware that your discernment and lack of peace are warning you not to move forward and enter into the wrong relationship.

No matter where you fall on the love, dating, and relationship spectrum, we should experience great peace while single and exude great wisdom in relationship building.

Selah—Why are you afraid to love again? How can you use your past mistakes as a learning tool so that you don't repeat those mistakes and end up disappointed or broken-hearted again?

Simple Prayer

Father, I thank you for always being with me and never leaving my side, even as I step out in faith to love again. I ask that you increase my discernment and help me to trust in you and the Holy Spirit's leadership in all my love, dating, and relationship choices. Have your way, Lord. In Jesus' name, Amen.

Scripture Reflection

Psalms 73:26 (AMPCE)

My flesh and my heart may fail, but God is the Rock and firm Strength of my heart and my Portion forever.

When you meditate on this scripture, what do you believe the Lord is speaking to your heart?

....

....

....

....

....

....

....

....

Trusting God's Timing

Psalm 37:3-5 (AMPC)

> *Trust (lean on, rely on, and be confident) in the Lord and do good; so shall you dwell in the land and feed surely on His faithfulness, and truly you shall be fed. Delight yourself also in the Lord, and He will give you the desires and secret petitions of your heart. Commit your way to the Lord [roll and repose each care of your load on Him]; trust (lean on, rely on, and be confident) also in Him and He will bring it to pass.*

God's timing is always perfect, even when it doesn't seem or feel perfect. Most times, it feels like God is late. Have you ever felt like God was too early in answering your prayers? Probably not!

It's normal to feel as if your prayers are delayed and hindered or even question whether God heard you at all.

Manifestation is never overnight, especially when it comes to our greatest heart's desires. A godly marriage is not a lofty prayer request and requires time to prepare both the husband and the wife to answer such an awesome calling.

Be encouraged that you are on the right path as long as you continue IN and WITH God. As long as you continue to give God your best, you can trust that he will take care of you. You don't have to be perfect; just do your best. None of us are perfect in our walk with Christ.

Think of Hannah, Noah, Abraham, and Elizabeth from the Bible. They had to all wait more than what anyone would consider a reasonable amount of time to get the manifestation of their prayers. They each needed to trust God when all signs told them to believe their senses over their faith.

Although they each had to wait a long time, what do they all have in common? Answered prayers. Desires made manifest. Dreams and visions given by God became a reality. Noah wasn't even asking for anything, but God still required him to be in faith against all odds, specifically for the plans and purposes of God.

What is God's plan for you? I can promise you that he has a great plan for your life. There is great purpose in your singleness. There is great purpose in your future marriage. Don't give up, and continue to hope against hope.

When the saints above hoped against all hope they didn't only manifest a partial answer to prayer or a barely-enough response from heaven. They received answers to prayer at very high levels of glorious manifestation. Abraham became the father of our faith. Hannah gave birth to the great Prophet Samuel. Noah and his family were the only ones to survive, along with animal life on the one-of-a-kind ark that took 100 years to build. And Elizabeth gave birth to John the Baptist. I don't believe it's a coincidence that these stories came with long periods of waiting. These are only a few examples God has given us to reveal patient endurance and how he determines how long an individual's waiting season is.

Woman of God, even though it feels as if God is late, he isn't. He will answer your prayer in your due season of harvest, and you will reap (Galatians 6:9).

Reflective Bible Study:

Read through these Bible characters' stories, Abraham, Hannah, Noah, and Elizabeth, and prayerfully consider what the Lord wants you to glean from each example. Write down what you believe God is saying to you about the wait and his timing. As you continue to wait, revisit this reflective study and remind yourself of God's personal promises and words of encouragement to you.

Simple Prayer

Lord, I believe I have all the patience and endurance I need to remain in faith for my desire for marriage. I ask that you would reveal to me how you want me to prepare and serve in your kingdom while I wait with expectancy. In Jesus' name, Amen.

Getting Better with Time

1st Peter 5:10 (AMPCE)

And after you have suffered a little while, the God of all grace [Who imparts all blessing and favor], Who has called you to His [own] eternal glory in Christ Jesus, will Himself complete and make you what you ought to be, establish and ground you securely, and strengthen, and settle you.

The longer you remain single, the stronger and more settled you should be in your faith for marriage. This statement may seem contradictory as most people's experience is the exact opposite. The longer they are single, the weaker they become in faith, and the more they begin to doubt God, make wrong decisions with men, and become bitter towards both God and men. This is an unfortunate misunderstanding of how your life with Christ should look.

Since you are a woman who spends time in prayer and study, your relationship with God should continually grow. Your personal revelations and confirmations from the Lord should increase and multiply. There should be an abundance of Bible stories and prophetic scriptures that speak to your heart very deeply, confirming God's will and plan for your life.

Additionally, since you are a woman who obeys the Holy Spirit's leadership and promptings, you should serve God's people with fervency and zeal. The love of God should so fill your heart that it easily flows out into the lives of those you are called to. This means you should experience a great fulfillment that only comes from true service and commitment to operating in your authentic calling, giftings, and anointing.

Since you are a woman of faith, you should be experiencing increasing levels of blessings as you live by faith and continually obtain favor, breakthrough, promotion, and answered prayers (Romans 1:17). The longer you are in faith, the more you learn how faith works. The more you begin to witness how faith operates, the more you learn how to use your faith in living the life God designed for you to live when he brought forth your life.

The sounds of the voices of doubt and fear, the negative influences and opinions of others, and the fiery darts thrown by the enemy are no match for your strong spirit of faith and commitment to believing God's Word. There is no way your faith can grow weak when you grow spiritually and continue to progress because you live by faith and walk with Christ. This doesn't mean that your life is perfect. It means that you live a life of faith, a life focused on and in submission to the kingdom's way of living. That includes perseverance, endurance, and fortifying your faith through the Word and personal relationship with God.

Does it now make sense that the longer you are single, the stronger you should be in faith? A bitter woman doesn't become that way overnight. Slowly but surely, she begins to give ear to the lies of Satan, the confusion of trying to be like the world instead of living an uncommon life for Christ, or the desperation that is birthed when the desire begins to consume her mind and heart. She may have had her heart broken repeatedly and has now become jaded by love. She may have been zealous for God but was let down by another unanswered prayer for something else in her life of great importance. She may set conditions and limitations for God that were not met, and therefore she has given up hope.

I do not want this for you, Woman of God. As the scripture says in 1st Peter 5:10, "you will suffer only a little while, but then the Holy Spirit will strengthen you and settle your faith," turning you into a formidable woman of faith. The years of faith lessons, personal prophetic words, dreams and visions, and the many moments of biblical confirmations you have received will solidify your faith. Nothing will be able to move you from your firm stance of belief, faith, and trust in God.

Faith Challenge:

Start putting together your war chest and fight the good fight of faith over the next 30 days. Take some time and write down every faith project or moment when you had to depend on God, and he came through for you. Write down every prayer that has already been answered beyond what you could fathom to ask. Go back through your prayer journal and remind your- self of the dreams, visions, and prophetic words the Lord has given you personally about marriage. If you have ever been prophesied to or if a teaching spoke to your heart deeply about marriage, write those instances down as well. Once you are done compiling all of these things, you should see a pattern. What has the Lord been consistently saying about your desire for marriage?

Simple Prayer

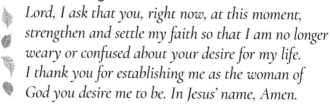

Lord, I ask that you, right now, at this moment, strengthen and settle my faith so that I am no longer weary or confused about your desire for my life. I thank you for establishing me as the woman of God you desire me to be. In Jesus' name, Amen.

The Blessing in The Wait

Hebrews 10:23-25 (NLT)

Let us hold tightly without wavering to the hope we affirm, for God can be trusted to keep his promise. Let us think of ways to motivate one another to acts of love and good works. And let us not neglect our meeting together, as some people do, but encourage one another, especially now that the day of his return is drawing near.

Waiting for God to answer your prayer for marriage can sometimes feel excruciating. However, there is a blessing in the waiting season that will lead to much joy, peace, and even contentment if you take full advantage of your season of singleness, enjoying all this season has to offer that will change forever once you are married.

The passage listed above refers to the waiting season of Christ's second return. Its wisdom can be applied in any situation where we are waiting on a personal promise from God to be fulfilled. As we wait, holding firmly to hope and believing in our trustworthy and reliable God, we should be busy living a blessed life of love and service.

There are friends, family, and acquaintances to share love with all around us. It's amazingly fulfilling to bless your neighbors with a get-well basket if they are feeling sick, treat a homeless person to a couple of nights stay at a nearby hotel, or send a thank you note to your boss, even if they are undeserving.

An abundance of joy and peace is obtained when you reach out to that family member you haven't spoken to in a while and take them out for lunch. Or plan a weekend visit with your nieces and nephews to spend time getting to know them while sharing kindness and love. Taking time to call an elderly family member who lives out of state brightens their day and provides a sense of fulfillment that only comes from investing in relationships.

There is also the blessing of having a church family to encourage you and provide support in this season, so you never feel utterly alone. You know you're not alone because even if you don't get the invitation for the holidays, you can create an invitation and host a gathering that brings other unmarried women together from your church to fellowship, laugh, and pray with each other.

There are other blessings to enjoy in this season that will disappear altogether once you are married, such as sleeping in and having the entire bed to yourself. You don't have to share covers, deal with snoring, or someone getting up earlier than you to get ready for work. You are free to make all your choices and decisions (as led by Holy Spirit, of course) on your own, without running them past your spouse or hoping they get on board with your idea.

If you do not yet have children, you have all the time in the world to work on any project you desire and set a schedule to your liking. You're free to travel, socialize, go to the spa or go on a weekend trip without the concern of childcare or finding family-friendly excursions.

You don't have to shave your legs if you don't want to. You don't have to cook or create meals if you don't feel like it. You can nap or sleep late in the mornings whenever you choose.

While you are waiting is the time to enjoy this season of freedom as much as possible. Your marriage will also be amazing, but your lifestyle will drastically change. If you struggle with finding the blessings in this season, ask God to help you. He will. He wants you to be joyful, peaceful, and content during the wait.

Selah—What do you enjoy the most about your single season? What are the benefits that you can appreciate as an unmarried woman?

Simple Prayer

Father, help me to enjoy this season of total devotion to you as a single woman. Show me how I can maximize this season and obtain the most incredible blessings during The Wait. In Jesus' name, Amen.

What To Do While You Wait

Ephesians 5:15-16 (AMPCE)

Look carefully then how you walk! Live purposefully and worthily and accurately, not as the unwise and witless, but as wise (sensible, intelligent people), Making the very most of the time [buying up each opportunity], because the days are evil.

*E*ven though your wait for marriage may be longer than you anticipated, the time you spend as a single woman is never wasted. From a kingdom perspective, your days should be filled with purposeful living. There is much to do in these last days, from experiencing the fullness of God's blessing on your life to making as many disciples as possible, winning souls into the kingdom of God.

The first priority in any Christian's life should be spending time to grow closer to God and learning more about his will and his ways. We as humans will never fully comprehend the depths of who the Almighty is in totality, yet there is much he will reveal to us about who he is as we walk and talk with him daily. You have the opportunity to get lost in the presence of God and fill your life with intimate, uninterrupted moments with the Holy Spirit, moments that will not be possible once you have a family.

You can learn more about how God loves you as his precious daughter and grow in the personal revelation of what it means to truly be loved by your Abba Father. You can grow in understanding how God loves all of his children when you serve, give and observe people through the eyes of God, the very lens of love. When you study the scriptures, you don't have to hurry through a lesson because of the demands of a husband and children. Instead, you can take your time and fully dive into a Bible story or person who interests you the most, dissecting every bit of spiritual truth to maximize growth and teaching to others.

We are all called to make disciples of Christ. Still, when you are free to explore the various opportunities available for operating in your gift, you can fine-tune your ministry and hone in on those God is sending you to, specifically. Your ministry message and method will be developed as you take risks and operate boldly in your calling, stepping out in faith using your spiritual gifts and talents. Nothing is more fulfilling than making a real impact in the lives of those individuals you are called to serve as only you can. This is a tangible benefit to redeeming the time in this season—accessing that fulfillment that gives birth to peace and contentment.

In both your personal endeavors and your ministry, there are opportunities to experience the highest level of blessing accessible to you, which requires both exposure and faith. Now is the time to place yourself in new environments that stretch you mentally, professionally, and socially so that the Lord can reveal another level of life and living you didn't even know existed. During these moments of exposure, you stretch your faith and belief, allowing you to take hold of a bigger vision, pursuing a greater blessing so that you can be a greater blessing to others.

Redeeming the time is not about filling your days with busy work or keeping yourself distracted from your desire for marriage. It's about using every second, minute, and hour intentionally, maximizing your life on this earth. Redeeming your time means you understand there is no time to waste and that you cannot get back anytime you spend on frivolous, pointless endeavors, conversations, or relationships. Yet when you redeem your time in a manner that is pleasing to God, the wonderful fruits of patience, peace, joy, contentment, and fulfillment are obtained.

Selah—Can you honestly say that you have been redeeming your time as a wise woman? What types of activities, people, or environments have been getting the best of your time?

Simple Prayer

Father, I ask for greater wisdom in how to spend my time, making the most of every moment and opportunity. Help me to recognize those things that are stealing or wasting my time so that I may live a more fruitful and fulfilling life in your presence and your perfect will. In Jesus' name, Amen.

Day 29

God's Perfect Match

Ephesians 2:10 (AMPCE)

For we are God's [own] handiwork (His workman-ship), recreated in Christ Jesus, [born anew] that we may do those good works which God predestined (planned beforehand) for us [taking paths which He prepared ahead of time], that we should walk in them [living the good life which He prearranged and made ready for us to live].

There is someone for everyone. There is a man out there who is your perfect match; likewise, you are his perfect choice in more ways than you can imagine. This fact may be hard to believe because your belief is based on your limited experiences. You may not see an abundance of spiritually strong and physically fine men of God who are single and respectfully pursuing a godly relationship. You may not be surrounded by mighty men of valor who pray, teach and live holy lives to the glory of God.

Additionally, you may have had a front-row seat to another woman's life who claimed to be sold-out-for-Christ, yet never got married or had children. You may witness Christian women all around you who are engaged or married but who live sinful lives and could care less about honoring God in their daily choices or with their bodies. You may have also witnessed women compromise and claim to be blissfully married to the man who was "not-what-they-wanted-but-what-they-needed." Perhaps you have shared some of these sentiments with other women of God.

Yet, when we consult the Word of God, at no point is there a limit placed on God when it comes to love and marriage. Ephesians 2:10 tells us that there is a good life that God himself has prepared and made ready for us to live. If God's original intention for men and women was to be fruitful and multiply (by getting married and having children), doesn't it stand to reason that the good life he prearranged for you would include the husband and children your heart so deeply desires? Why would a family be excluded from this good life? Why would God want you to marry someone who will not come alongside you to serve God together? Or someone who cannot teach your children godliness, or even someone you are not even physically attracted to?

The quiet season of singleness is no time to allow doubt to chip away at your faith. It's no time to allow the confusing words of others to crush your hopes and dreams. It's no time to focus on what you see with your eyes more than on the unseen, the spiritual realm filled with possibilities (2 Kings 6:17).

God has a perfect match for you. You haven't encountered him yet, but keep believing, keep trusting, and pressing forward in faith. God's plan for your future is filled with love and joy, regardless of your past. His plan for your future will provide a great testimony for the world to see. Don't be like the children of Israel who died in the wilderness because their hearts hardened toward God. Be like Joshua, strong and courageous, believing against all odds that you can and will possess your own personal promised land!

Selah—What can you honestly say is the biggest enemy of your faith? How can you adjust your life to address and remove this enemy so your faith may be strengthened?

Simple Prayer

Father, help me to view my future through a lens of faith and comprehend the depths of your love for me in a greater magnitude. In Jesus' name, Amen.

Scripture Reflection

Luke 1:37 (AMPCE)

> *For with God, nothing is ever impossible, and no word from God shall be without power or impossible of fulfillment.*

When you meditate on this scripture, what do you believe the Lord is speaking to your heart?

....

....

....

....

....

....

....

....

Day 30

There SHALL Be a Performance!

Luke 1:45 (KJV)

And blessed is she that believed: for there shall be a performance of those things which were told her from the Lord.

When the Lord makes you a personal promise or reveals his desired future for your life, your only job is to believe. Think about it like this: To be in the position to get a personal word from the Lord or a vision/dream from heaven would mean that you are a woman of prayer. You are a woman who studies the Word and does your best to honor God with your life.

Therefore, when God reveals his plans to you, you don't have to work or earn the performance of that plan; all you have to do is believe what the Lord has revealed to you.

That's all Mary had to do. That's all her cousin Elizabeth had to do. When the Lord gave them an impossible vision that HE was responsible for bringing to pass, they only had to believe, and it was done. The plan for their lives was performed supernaturally.

You've heard the saying: "God didn't promise anyone a spouse," haven't you? Well, if the truth is told, no one knows exactly what God has promised to any individual unless they were right there with that person in their prayer closet. When you were on your face in the presence of God and the Holy Spirit spoke to your heart, was anyone in the room with you? When you were fasting and praying for your future husband, did you do so secretly or surrounded by others? You were alone in your quiet prayer and worship time with the Lord when he spoke to you about your future husband and marriage.

God makes personal promises to all his children if they take the time to live for him, following his ways and worshipping him in spirit and truth. We are not required to live a perfect Christian life by any means, but when we give our honest effort to live according to the Word and honor God with our lives, God speaks to us individually about what he desires for our present and future seasons of life.

Let God take the reigns of your life and decide to submit totally to his plan. Do not try to intervene or take control of your singleness. Indeed, you will have quiet seasons in your singleness journey when you are not dating anyone or receiving attention from the right type of man. There will be days when the wait feels more excruciating than others. There will even be brief moments when you question what the Lord has shown you.

You are human. But, as long as these moments are brief and fleeting and you continue on the path of total surrender to God, you will see the promise manifest in your life!

Increase Your Belief Challenge:

Take a day or two to review the entries in your last three prayer journals (or go back at least five years). Compile every revelation, prophetic word, or dream (re-writing each individual sentence/paragraph) into a new sheet/document. Include the specific scriptures those revelations were based upon. Then, read the entire manuscript out loud as one lengthy manifesto of God's personal promise to you about your future husband/marriage. On the next page, write down each scripture that has spoken to your heart deeply concerning your desire for marriage through the years. Read these out loud as faith declarations for the next 30 days. Your faith and hope should be significantly increased and solidified through this process!

Simple Prayer

Lord, I ask that you help me to remain in faith no matter the circumstance and believe what you have revealed to my heart concerning my future husband/ marriage. Give me fresh revelation in the Word to help solidify my faith in your personal promise. In Jesus' name, Amen.

Appendix

Confidence and Faith—Building Scriptures for Godly Marriage

These are a compilation of scriptures pertaining specifically to godly marriage, your desires being fulfilled, faith, prayer, God's timing, and instructions for Christian husbands and wives. Read each scripture in multiple translations to get a personal revelation from heaven. Be sure to write down everything the Lord speaks to your heart and allow the Word of God to encourage your faith greatly!

John 17:17

Isaiah 40:8

Matthew 4:4

Hebrews 6:18

Psalms 37:4-5

Proverbs 10:24

Matthew 6:33

Psalms 20:4

John 15:7-8

Ephesians 3:20

Luke 1:37

Psalms 21:2

Psalms 145:19

1 John 5:14-15

Mark 11:23

Luke 1:45

Proverbs 13:12

Matthew 5:8

Matthew 9:29

Matthew 19:26

Matthew 7:8

Proverbs 3:5

Psalms 27:14

Luke 8:15

Jeremiah 29:5-7

Genesis 1:28

Genesis 9:7

Genesis 2:18

Ephesians Chapter 5

Genesis 18:19

Genesis 2:24

Malachi 2:13-16

1 Timothy 5:11-14

Hebrews 13:4

Proverbs 18:22
Colossians 3:18-19
1 Peter 3:7
Deuteronomy 28:4
Proverbs 19:14
Deuteronomy 24:5
Deuteronomy 28:11
Deuteronomy 28:63

Ephesians 2:10
Philippians 2:13
Psalms 139:16
Jeremiah 29:11
Romans 8:28
Psalms 40:8
Proverbs 16:3
Romans 12:2

Bible Love Stories and Power Couples

Adam & Eve, Genesis 2
Isaac & Rebekah, Genesis 24-27
Jacob & Rachel, Genesis 29-30
Elkanah & Hannah, 1 Samuel 1-2
Zechariah & Elizabeth, Luke 1-2
Aquila & Priscilla, Acts 18-19
Joseph & Mary, Matthew Chapter 1

About the Author

Sarita A. Foxworth is a Bible Teacher, Author & Retreat Host for single Christian women. Her life's mission is teaching how to date smarter, grow in faith, and operate in high levels of purpose and calling. She does this through her books, coaching programs, events, and luxury retreats.

In 2010 Sarita began serving and teaching women at her home Bible study groups focusing on health, beauty, love, and life's purpose. The group grew over the next four years, and testimonies poured in. Women were getting married, growing in their confidence and understanding of who they were as women, and stepping into their life's purpose and calling.

To increase her skillset in helping women spiritually, personally, and professionally she attended The Coaching and Positive Psychology Institute in 2014, receiving certification as a Personal and Executive Life Coach. Shortly after graduation, she started her Christian life coaching business, offering personal coaching programs, luxury retreats, and self-publishing programs for new authors.

Since then, she has launched a worldwide ministry of fasting and prayer and has written over twelve books curated for single Christian women and new authors. She also teaches regular Bible studies to help women practically apply the truth of God's Word to daily living.

Sarita actively works to connect like-minded women of faith and create a responsive community of support and love while challenging women to make a significant impact in this generation to the glory of God. She invites you to join this beautiful community by subscribing to her YouTube channel or following her Instagram posts and conversations. It would be her honor to serve as your mentor and life coach. You can also connect with Sarita by signing up on her email list at www.SaritaFoxworth.com.

Next Steps

CONNECT WITH ME

This book was powerful, wasn't it?! The Holy Spirit was integral to the writing process. I'd LOVE to hear how it's blessed your life! Please share your review on Amazon. com. You can also share a cute picture of this book with your audience and tag me on Instagram (@Sarita.foxworth), so I can find it!

The best way to connect with me is by joining my email list at www.SaritaFoxworth.com. I send out evening devotionals and weekly encouragement and have a private "Ask Sarita" email series to regularly engage with real women like you.

Want to meet me at a live event, prayer meeting, or retreat? Once you're on the email list, you will be the first to know upcoming event details and get first-access invitations to virtual and live events.

GO DEEPER

If you have been struggling with doubt and fear concerning your singleness or the season of waiting, go to my Youtube channel (Sarita A. Foxworth) and check out a Bible study series I created called: *God Wants You Married*. This series includes a Bible study notes download with over 30 faith-inducing scriptures about kingdom marriage.

BOOK SHOP

All books are available worldwide for purchase directly from the Love & Miracles Book Boutique. Whether you need help hearing from God in prayer, understanding your prophetic anointing, or learning and loving the woman you are, there is a book that will greatly bless your life!

You can also purchase a group book order inclusive of bulk discount pricing from the L & M Publishing website (www.lmpublishing.co). There are also beautiful gifts to choose from that will wow your audience!

Printed in Great Britain
by Amazon

36618565R00076